Danke Schoen

Danke Schoen

Alexandria Ashford

THE POETRY PRESS
2010

HOLLYWOOD, CALIFORNIA

Published by
THE POETRY PRESS
of Press Americana

the press of

Americana:
The Institute for the Study of
American Popular Culture
7095-1240 Hollywood Boulevard
Hollywood, CA 90028

http://www.americanpopularculture.com

© 2010 Americana: The Institute for the Study of American Popular Culture and Alexandria Ashford

Library of Congress Cataloging-in-Publication Data

Ashford, Alexandria.
 Danke schoen : poems / by Alexandria Ashford.
    p. cm.
 ISBN 978-0-9789041-0-4 (alk. paper)
 I. Title.

PS3601.S5426D36 2010
811'.6--dc22
                            2010032517

For Mary Eliza

I have only what I remember.

-W.S. Merwin

Table of Contents

I   1

Elegy in Broken Stanzas   2
Wake   4
May-Ellen at Her Son's Grave   5
Loss   6
West Cape   7
Peach Tree   9
Art   10
Portrait of Longing in Three Parts   11
Victrola and Sunset   12
Buttahatchie June   13
Ode to a Farmhouse   14
Embryo   15
Leroy   17
Afterglow   18
Mon Fille   19
Milagro (A Prayer for Nine Night)   20

II   21

For Eliza on Her Birthday   22
Of Newness, Of Ghosts   23
Vertigo   24
Harlem Manifesto   25
Tanque   27
December Rock   28
Bien-Aimé   29
To Sifa With Love   30
Kiss   31
Prayer   32
Summer Solstice   33
Gravity   34
Braids   36
Lisbon   37
Prima Donna (or what you will)   38
Wanting   39

III   41

Danke Schoen   42
To Myself on the Eve of My Miscarriage   43
Casualty   44
Outskirts   45
Woman   46
Suicide   47
Approaching Abinadab   48
Poem In Which I Am Only Hinting   49
For My Mother, a West Indian   50
Mulatto   51
Down at the Crossroads   52
Azuza Woman   53
Sestina   54
Pseudonym   56
Etta Sings the Blues   57
Hymn for Defilee   58

I

*Hear me out: that which you call death
I remember.*

-Louise Gluck

Elegy in Broken Stanzas
               For Corey

A.R. Leak and Sons Funeral Home
when the sun went down, Moma
Liz wore her biggest blackest hat,
rolled her chubby yellow hand across
your face over and over again, groaning
something none of us could decode:
December cake: white phosphorus: casket talk.
            I may only ever hint at those vast brown eyes flecked
            with mulatto green and Chicago sun—by lighting
            candles as is custom, humming that song
            you sang in church. I'll write as long as I can
            of the broken slant in your nose; your love for sweet-dirt,
            as if to give you back to yourself. If I could give
            you anything back, it would be summer 1995.
            You were eight then. The age of tonka
trucks and bare feet, black bayou and luck in four leaf clovers.
When the sun was highest and hottest in the sky, I told you
stories under the grandfather tree, kept you safe from bumble-
bees and sunburn. Held your hand when we crossed the street in search
of honeysuckle. Admonished you as a "big boy." We couldn't have
known that death was so possible. Like scraped knees. Shoe polish.
A polecat.
How ignorant I was,
Still am: Language fails me,
        But I wanted to
write this for you. *I wanted*
to cry a while and write this
for you. To once more
hold your hand as you cross
the road—older—this time into something
wider; something tall as the way
Mahalia sang. And even here, I fall short.
            I cannot cross with you. Help you dodge the snapperfish,
            choose the shallowest pond. Instead, I choose a soft clean
            voice in which to pray, listen to my love, thick with
            fragrance cross the void. Every day, your face is my votive:
            that grin—open shimmer—that oh-so-fly black Chicago
            boy bad with the basketball. Darling you. September

evenings, I wait for you at the storm cellar til the hollyhock burns my nose. I can still see those great big eyes sparkle, your scraped knees matted with fescue, boy blood clean and blue as India ink.

Wake
    For CK

Your body was cold by then
    like frozen earth, laid flat. A fir
        tree in its year of death.

There was a crescent of cold
    around you, quiet and secret
        as a falling star.

My whispers carried across
    the wide room like long slivers
        of moon, bending to hug the dark.

And I was there in pieces
    clasping dreams of hemlock
        and next lifetimes.

I have come now to glean
    the fields of nothingness, wear
        midnight upon my shoulders.

To do the waking
    you will not do again
        in this world.

May-Ellen at her Son's Grave

Dirt clings to the shovel.
The mother, a skeleton herself,
weeps obscenities—the dark
blue breath that hovers close to her face.
Her head hangs low,
a cloud threatening rain.
She wails to her dead boy:
butterfly with tin wings:
muscadine past its summer.

Loss

Like the span
Of gold-veined lightning,
Moonshine thick
As tree trunks,
Cannot be written,
Only felt.

After Arthur Golden

West Cape
In Memoriam

This year the cape has changed.
Green is anchored deeper
than the water itself.
Sky looks so much like sea
even the egrets are confused,

just the way you'd want it.

I spent this winter envisioning you
back at the vineyard, fingers sticky
with "blueberry surprise,"
back glued to the longest branch
of white-blooded birch.

I am twelve again
waiting for you to run into
the meadow, that Cheshire
Cat of a smile on your face,
so we can race to that cliff
on the north end, the one with
vines and foxgloves covering
the lighthouse, whitewashed and grand
against a distance of gunmetal blue.

It was there that we laughed until
our stomachs hurt, took our
first sips of moonshine
(my uncle's brew)
smashed fireflies and rubbed
our skin sore so that we too might
glow.

That was years before the deacons
clothed in black. The summer
covered in moths, weeds,
cicadas. The cemetery singing:

Your loss is my gain.

At the west end of this square
a headstone floraled, faded
and dreaming. Your name
etched deliberately into
stone. Years curved in calligraphy:

       1984-2005

The small line between
years meant to symbolize
a whole life: the
boy who shared my
summers draped in magic.
As if you were no vaster
than that small space
between the years,
the life you lived
little more than language
unfolding itself on a rock.

Peach Tree

We named it Eliza. A name that
means *my God is a vow*

but only because it grew in your
backyard, crooked and narrow

as sugar cane. And quiet—
like hidden laughter that

does not want to be found. Now
I expect this tree to become

some version of you. That the leaflets
will grow greener, the peaches fleshed

like blushing virgin fronds.
I expect the wildness to subside,

the center to be pure.
Tell me what's at the heart

of this tree that yields peaches
full of worms. What does this say

of you? The girl who slept in pansies,
ran free in fields of black-eyed susans.

That love made you fragile, timid,
and now only worms remain.

Art

The vinyl record cracks, screeches.
We wait to hear its lazy summer
prelude. Sunlight stripes the room:
a zebra in closeted, brown wind,
almost a checkerboard against
the windows sullied with fingerprints.
Illuminated specks of dust suspend
in thick, syrupy air.

My grandma takes her walking stick,
plunks the heavy wood against the table.
Her body moves free with that thin,
cotton gown. It knows no caution, only
the contours of her body. Only that
It won't dare get in her way.
The sun-sweet melody plays—
becomes one with our bones.

We dance slavery, servitude, World Wars.
Hot days in the cotton field,
on our knees in cool, black soil
searching for sweet potatoes.
We sing cherry blossoms, blood,
and sweet, apple pie—a slow boil
beneath the candied sun. We think
strength, courage, survival against
this ripe, southern sky. We learn
each time the record stops and starts again:
the art of ending—
the art of beginning.

Portrait of Longing in Three Parts

I
The willingness to slough off
myself is here. The night is lip-
synching, pristine sadist that it is;
likes to see me suffer.

Day leaves me browned around the edges
but learned: sparrow, daisy, hollyhock
mallow—this is your song.

II
Themes I can't explain are at work:
the law that governs longing,
that has so skillfully hidden itself
beneath the peat and debris of time.
Its array of minutes and hours.

Nothing makes more sense now
than detachment: separate girl
from South; South from blue-green
estuary, stone white whiskey
and dune swales. Longing then
becomes a stretching of syllabic
light, flitty curl of the tongue.

III
No one can stop the way the breezes
bend here. Stop the grotesque
from taking place. This is the swamp:
bayou: the place where I was formed.
Birthright, *what are you*, covered in after-
birth? You have forgotten to push me out
into the real. I am still a waking dream,
an event on the helm. And right beside me
is blue-white God, who is now dividing me
into equal portions: One for the living.
One for the dead.

Victrola and Sunset

Late afternoon we drink sweet
tea, speak of yesterday's rain—

bows of lightning bringing us back
as the victrola screeches onward.

We know this slow, dark tune,
what it means for girls our color.

Still, we keep up appearances.
This party of lost wills and dolor.

I ask, as if from reticence, where
the tune ends on the ebony spindle-

wheel of the victrola, yawning
its story through our ears.

And I know the answer lies
in this rum-colored sunlight,

the roof's stalwart, turpentine sway
—a stagnate, speckled pond

that has worn a hole in your will.
A hole that is wide and never full,

cloaking the unfaithful mind
in a black as open and deep

as the snap-dragon distance
pulling slowly downward.

Buttahatchie June
For Mr. Juan Franco

Don't be afraid to flirt
with death. *Dive,*
as if for a life,
blue-black body
void of its ghost.
I'll see you on the way
back up, your bones
slender, white houses
athrob beneath a canopy
of skin. Skin that, above
all else, desires *air*.
It tingles, doesn't it?
The sound of river, *ending,*
washing over you like a myth
whose truth you cannot decipher.

Ode to a Farmhouse

No matter what you call it, there
it will be, laid out like a wide white line
parched and heavy and still like a cloud longing for rain.

> Fourteen children crossed its threshold
> hoping themselves away from plank walls,
> the turpentine roof. Some of them never came back. Others

>> still remain, ghosts of a place they longed
>> to escape. Like the geese that leave each autumn
>> in search of heat and food. I imagine it's the
> Keys they fly off to,

somewhere warm and full as a tongue.
Now the children return home like lost egrets
unfamiliar with the scenes that guided their youth: whiskey

> bottle sunsets, half-mooned midnight braided with hunger.
> The house leans west, entry crumbling like old laughter, frame
> withered as a drowned bird. They return now—arbitrarily—

>> to ceilings the color of shamrock, walls
>> Berlinesque in their ruin; piles of sheet-rock
>> stacked like tiny shipwrecks glowing
>> white as the gypsied twilight cloaking the
> newborn distance.

Embryo

I.

I learned to peel potatoes in reverse. The yellow first. Then the brown.
    This is how I justify racism. This is how I learn to hate them first.
        Throw them at me, your dirty words. I'll catch them on the backs
            of my hands.

The wind in Alabama is urgent, bleeding. How else could the earth show
    remorse for its lynch-mob sunsets, blood moons, beet-red music that
        is nothing if not ostensible? The sky waxes green, pregnant with
            storm. Everything here is
            subtext. Bullet.

When grandma wants to tell a story, she groans. Like the world opening
    upon itself, wordless. Succinct. The oppressed are unabashed. They
        learn it from the stars that burn themselves out. Open in flame.
            Forgotten—like slaves.
            Always forgotten.

After embers have died, they leave clues of the flame they were. *I was*
    golden, the ashes think. *I was blue.* Think of bones this way. They
        live beneath earths, under streams. White sepulchers. *I came*
            here beneath a ship. I
            lived under a sun. I cried.

II.

I am about to be born on a shore in Benin. The world outside me begs,
    Tongues curling, the scraped squeal of machetes grating, moaning a
        dying language. Slowly I make my way to your heart, rising
            like white heat and burning
            away like mid-evening fog.

Feel me stretching, the product of midnight, hot Nile river-bed, budding
       into smoke and sorrow. I am a coconut growing inside you, a
            cacophony of blue blood. Green vein of the body, forking and
                  pulsing, wild and red
                  as Haitian summer.

Outside me, sounds of goats protesting death. White entrails spill to the
       ground, chant *I am your future.* In one day, the thing you have fed
           will enter the world demanding. Nothing you pray will end
               it. With every word
                 you speak, it will stir.

Like all black magic that enters through a seed, slim as a fracture,
       venturing into the night of a womb. There it waits, deliberately as a
           cockerel after a long winter of waiting and hunger and loss.
               Clean as the drinking-gourd north,
                 rolling burial ground of the moon.

Leroy

At night you hang from the tree

outside my window, neck

snapped like a dandelion stem.

You must've been handsome

in your lifetime; in your early

twenties when you died.

And nothing's amiss besides

the neck. Even the eyes

seem lucent—bright as jewelfish.

I think: *you must've known.*

Then turn over in my bed.

Afterglow

Autumn sun has baked September
into the apple trees, and they shine
like vermilion clouds afloat
on kerosene. The weight

of the earth starts here, on a narrow
slice of wind between us and the hearth.
If we are searching for a burial place
then why not this cloud?

Entombment means many things:
cocooned silence before rain,
festooned blue sky cornered by the space
that warns against catastrophe.

The apples look blue beneath
this moonlight, its cool caress pulling
shadows across the tendrils
of our willow tree.

The sky is sliced in half
by a star that will not burn
out. The other half is black,
the darkness that comes

when light hides itself
from the world, leaving
ghosts of the world before,
afterglow of the dead.

Mon Fille
For my daughter

I have thought of you in my dreams
the inevitable slant of your father's forehead
the narrow fingernails passed down
from the women in my family
presenting themselves again through you.

I have dreamt of burnt orange fields you might have played in
of telling you the stories of your grandmother
who escaped charging bulls in the backlands
climbed pecan trees near the witching fields
learned the sorrows of girlhood between the thighs of lonely men.

I would have you remember (always)
whatever returns from oblivion
returns to find a voice:
the dead are not so far from us.

I would tell you in proverbs what your heart could not hold
give you in kisses the love too thick to speak
I offer you my beating heart, still warm
mon fille.

I dream often of you leaving my body:
furious red thick with the sin of my mistakes.
Some nights I see you riding a green truss of moonlight
brushing the stars from your hair—
mon fille.

Milagro (A Prayer for Nine Night)

Sleeping:
That's the way
I want to be found
At the hour
Of your death
When they come
To tell me
Of the shadowlands,
Kristallnacht miasma
Into which
You have surely
Passed.

II

Yes, you are loved. Why else this song?

-Adrienne Rich

For Eliza on Her Birthday

In October when the grief is thick, I remember those sun-spangled eyes,
the arms like sweet brown ribbon. The need and how it bled
through me like horse apple milk, onto the robes of your
motherhood. I remember the moon at its whitest peak
in the west, watching as it incandesced. Its glow
weaving a circle around the hearth. The song
you hummed after midnight:

> *Little baby, little child*
> *Close thee' eyes*
> *And rest awhile*
> *The sun will keep shinin'*
> *My love will not go*
> *There'll never be time*
> *When this is not so…*

And your smile on those nights
when the moon striped the room.
How it burned to know
you were mortal.

Of Newness, Of Ghosts
                For Shun

It was simple enough counting
stars: the porch post
thick slate
our names carved
in its body.
How did we live to be this young—
dandelion quills lit
by the flecks
of comets?
Now we barely recognize the ghosts
we are not.
How long before
we can say we've
learned everything
about nothing?
Supernova climbing a black wall
of clean sky,
green lights entering
us from the ground up
just like we belong
to them. Just like they knew
we'd come.
And all night the moon staring back at us
from years ahead.

Vertigo

I linger as if waiting
        for the world
to collapse,

                fall through like plans
                      ripe with purpose,
                best intention.

I have decided that
        we, my love,
are galaxies

                hinged on a black hole
                      left of center
                void of radius.

I want to tell you
        everything,
love you completely,

                if only the center
                    would hold
                without complaint,

let us be more than ash,
        flailing embers
pulsing with the intent

                of fire.

Harlem Manifesto

I'm feeling the leaflets
shiver in unison of drip-
drop melody: side slung
and half awake, midnight
wears a milk-glass
veil, a crooked smile
etched in miles of sister stars.

On the corner of 7th Street
the hoods stand near Alfie's
Corner Store inhaling jazz
and asphalt vapor, staring ocean
eyed at the out-of-towners,
and just for tonight are laying
off the booze.

In the pool hall, leather
clad papas are being
left breathless by a honey-
blue tune floating just
below the roof;
heavy blinds are slicing
up the moon, leaving
scattered strips of light
across checkered tiles.

The whole scene is fluid.
Just cool enough for my budding
senses to drink down. At twelve
I think I understand why all
these black folks are here.
I want to be the tune. The tiles.
The sliced up moon.
But not yet.

Then mother comes to steal me
from the magnetism, the reds
and blacks I'm breaking into.
And as we walk away, I see

one man. He has taken off
his boyhood and is glowing.
To me he is solid gold—
pink canary. And smooth
as Indian night.

Tanque
For Lionel

Bone blue
Portugal is a riddle:
lemonzest peony
yesteryear nostalgia.
Blood on brass
moonlight rewinds
to fashion bullets
in my veins.

        In retrospect (picture!)
        the moment when it was all
        over—the wonder of inversion,
        of you naked
        and fully human.

Friend, words do not
suffice. This is only
to say

I

    was

wrong.

December Rock

I've never seen a sky tilt quite like this one: a little north,
a little south, stretched across miles and miles
of plum bay. This was your piece of sky, blue-
gray and daring, bending against Lisbon's coast,
poppies furring its tip like a blonde coif. I like to think
you're out there in the beyond, folded in Viking
tales and China moon. I'm afraid you'll lose my
memory somewhere out there in the long gray
arms of eternity.

What shall I say now that words do not suffice? I remember
the way you loved walking barefoot on the rocks,
though I could never find much use for them, such
rootless, frivolous things. But this pebble, striped
pewter paradise, nestled on a ripe stretch of shore
must belong to you. This one, blue green kaleido-
scope, polished by December wind, surely belongs
to you.

Bien-Aimé

Your nails jagged
as cypress grooves

The big black irises
that swallow my whole body

I lay my heart at your feet
still beating

It is your memory, my love,
that I love.

To Sifa With Love

When I want to be sober
I watch you from my soapbox,
your pink pagne the color
of a summer bird, Bukavu
in its fullest spring equinox.
I can't tell you how many times
I've groaned about loss. Door
keys, earrings, loves. I see
your body raped and pillaged,
broke-down palace of a thing.
Then you raise your hands
like a moth reaching for starlight:
like clean hands on Sunday
reaching for the altar.

Kiss

From our steel-
Veined consciousness
The clouds come
Billowing in: open-
Blue in an agile erasure.
This is what is supposed
To happen when I
Cross the bridge,
Womb growing in
Seconds, like sea-scape
Beneath glass and ponds
Of blue whiskey. You
See how lovely I am
Or how dead. Not
Merely the touching
Of lips we were after,
But an excision
We have come to applaud
A blue green zip that will
One day measure us,
Size us up
As the aged
We have become.

Prayer

In Portugal, I trace your name
on the heartwood pews of Se Catedral
de Silves, staring skyward at angels
and demons carved in bronze.
This one holds a candle, watches
the beam left of it: a sun-striped world
that holds my dreams and his. I wait
for him to fly to his beloved
—yellow belladonna in her prime—
and long for his world
to move.

Summer Solstice

Orange-pink
morning star,
prickly panicles
beneath a fibrous dress.
Almond-eyed children
devour bagoong
por la tarde.
The wind whisks
purple petals:
jacaranda blooms.
Resin drips:
drip drip drop
upon a small dreaming head
daydreaming beneath
the flaming sky.

Gravity

Calabria is sleepy on this edge of Eastern
sky. Foccacia, plums, and paradise:
this autumn is silvered and sweet.
Along this beaten path we wander
in our old Sedan. You tell me of your
boyhood in blue flannel; tall grass;
ladybugs. In my head I see
my mother's lean, hungry legs drenched
in sweat—her straw hat laughing on Sunday
mornings.

Somewhere on the long stretch of road,
you were quiet. I stopped hearing
the ruckus of your breathy, wily chatter;
on the broken radio, we could
no longer hear the song. It felt like
my days in the yellow fields, grasping
at the flat clouds—their nearness
an imposter: my life on the back roads
growing up way too fast,

like when I chased a rainbow
to the edge of the county, thinking
I could hold another world inside my
bare hands. And when I couldn't
find it, I stilled myself from the
wishing and traded hope
for existence: for something
I could write down—explain to
people at dinner tables covered
in Georgian lace, crystal flutes of
Arabic tea.

As if the living had emptied
me out. As if time had carved
holes in my skin. I can hear
myself and no one else now: back
to the girl in the poppy fields;

back to the boy in blue
flannel.

Braids
For my sister

When you are old enough
you will learn this, she says
throwing synthetic hair over
one shoulder, a bobby pin
clamped down between
gapped teeth. Part the hair
into a square. *The trick*
is to learn when enough
is enough. Pull until
the strands almost break,
tight enough to raise
the scalp, pinpoint every
tiny follicle. *The trick*
is to know that it hurts.
Your client knows this
before she asks for braids.
She must wear them as a token
as a warrior his scars.

Lisbon

Here at the café, clouds
thick as paraffin above
us, you tell me of the speckled
birds in Rossio Square
that braid their songs into
the whistles of vagrants
on park benches, hair
stained with the fluid
of the city, semen of the night.
I tell you of the quiet that comes
only in rural towns you've never
seen that would scare the hell
out of any woman.
I tell you that a woman is a different
thing on the other side of the world—
bird gray with gold fever,
and smothered by her sky.

Prima Donna (or what you will)

I can hear the rumbling
(yes, your dreams are audible)
and I know that we're there
at that ridiculous crossroad
Golgotha: moon white and void.
Right before I go out and lose
myself forever and never
quite understand why you touched
me the way you did right before
leaving or why it took you so long
to do it. Before I ask you one
last time why things can't
be different and you exclaim

Only in a perfect world:

which is to say God,
slate blue fog before twilight
slim slot of earth near the Tiber
wet September midnight
in Piazza Navona when I
was so beautifully naïve
and you loved me.

Wanting
           For D

i want to

pick you up

clean you off

put you back

on the shelf

you fell from

make you:

RIGHT

make us:

RIGHT

again.

III

even grandmother's ghee
cannot mend
the delicate embroideries
of bone.

-Audre Lorde

Danke Schoen

Aprils when the world waxed lunar white, my grandmother
put up peach preserves. We listened to the popping
of the record as Wayne Newton sang
        Danke Schoen
        Darlin' Danke Schoen...
We could not have known those foreign words
meant *Thank you very much*. That they really meant
        Thanks pretty.
Had I known, I would've told him: *black girls aren't
pretty, Wayne. But we sure know how to survive.*
October fourteenths I drink bourbon and call to haints
the color of quillwort in dry season, the ugly blotch
of my ancestry in clear view. The bravery in me has been spent.
        My mind's not right.
No one told me that hope was ugly, trifling, and black:
like great grandmother Lizzie who drank moonshine
from a chipped glass and wore purple lace stockings
as holey-as-they-wanna-be and groaned negro spirituals
til my head sang and told stories of Job and how
he lost it all but won because he put one foot in front
of the other and kept walking when he should've lost
        his cotton-pickin' mind.
Still I wonder why I can't recognize disaster when I see
it. Why I didn't know what the hell Wayne Newton
was singing in that song as he crooned into our ears.
Why no one told me that hope is slow, dark
and painstaking as the night wind.
Indiscernible as a lucifered heart.

To Myself on the Eve of my Miscarriage

you
are the one
he will always
remember
let that be
enough.

Casualty

It was accidental, this weaving,
melding of fair and dark skin into
one motley orb.
               Endings are repeated histories
my grandmother said, but ours
was tragic, beautifully original.
Now there is only what we
have done to one another,
conch shell of a life we have
slept with and owned.
               We ended on this highway,
a straight line from Gulfport
to the Riviera: sand dumped
over a mangrove swamp, world
of buried memoir.
               We are fools not to ask
how it went so fast. Why each
time my husband pulls his fingers
along my skin like a sleep-sharpened
eel, I wish—always—for the yellow
Judas Sundays I lived in your
sea.

Outskirts

At the core of everything
lies the dust you run from

each day. Every bent
breeze leads back,

the same green thunder,
the same gentility you learn

from birth. From the mother
who whispers: *this way, child.*

Lean this way. Or from the father
whose thoughts are hidden away,

locked within an encrypted bottle
of cheap liquor, its poison

hidden beneath a bourbon
veil. He has learned how

to hit your mother from his
own father: a man prickled

with the fear that manhood
was nothing without anger.

The swelling of words
in his throat, curling lips

that speak the word *bitch*—
his very tongue formed inside

a womb black with
the nervousness of youth,

fear of the cave life forms around
un-married girls from the outskirts.

Woman

Those women
who hide in the crotches
of men, who like
to roam long and search
wide—I was with you
and in you from cross-wise
to never-ending infinite.
It is never easy.
Never what you thought
or first believed:
not the blue damask of sea foam
or the bright red of cherry moon.
That would be too easy.
We are women because we love
well. We know that without
what we give, life would stop living.
Moonlight was never intended
To be understood, but rather to drift hungrily
Over the shoulder. Geishan. Hetaeran.
To kiss you good night, give you
A halo you would never receive any
other way. Because the universe
in all its green commodity and black
ebony fire is still ours. Still breathes
in our wombs, at our backs.

Suicide

Crimson lies at her feet in scant,
distorted streams.

Her fingers are cherry bum rods,
Scratching, purring.

She was right to slit her wrists.
Women like us don't cry.

Approaching Abinadab

The sun calls back   from the east
Yellowish   like July bread
Dandelion quill   inverted with hunger.

Summer starts where   the world has failed itself
The deep brown space   where need screams
The void closes   where the geese begin:

The sky. Oh, the sky.

All this as the moon   stares back from years ahead
Perching chickadee   humming to Sirius's belly
Itself a figment   jealous of the sun—

That it can be light   and heat at once
Must be dark beneath   God's underside
On the ribbon   where truths converge:

water	river	blood	birth
fire	ash	slave	tree

Call it out until the world makes sense.

Poem In Which I Am Only Hinting

You could call it the same name
You call the black ribbon that ties
Itself around the heart after disaster,
A cunning treatise that wants to fool
You into thinking it's normal.
Think of the way skin
Peels after it is burned, crinkled over
In fright: how this stings.
Think of the way a baby can bleed
Straight through you and clean
down the center before you
Realize the obvious: *a life lived
Inside you*: Tragedy. Think
Of those you love scalding
You with reckless abandon.
Think of your knees giving way,
Like a marriage ending, a dream
Settling away on a mist just
Beyond your reach. Think
Of the lengths you'll go through
to explain one tiny word:
Pain. And in the end, only
Hint at it.

For My Mother, a West Indian

The Jamaica you know is stretched clean
and tight against the Atlantic, its own ode
to the West unfolding in yellow hills, juniper
branches, conchers on the decks of loud
gray ships.

What I know of Jamaica is the world collapsing,
my great aunt diving into the hotel fountain for pennies;
my mother saying *I must see that place before I die.* She
believes that being West Indian is somehow different
from being black, until the slums wrap themselves
around her, the sullied windows of shanty-towns refusing
to be iridescent.
>   Young girls turning cartwheels
>   for *fitty cents please. One dollar*
>   *for a guava. A dollar extra*
>   *I be yours.*

In the pastel green taxi, a coffee-skinned Virgin Mary
sways back and forth on the dash, smacking yellow
rosary beads in a rhythmic prayer, the sound
of Jamaican rum swishing with each hump in the road.
Mother mentions the name of German Aunt Mischka,
her half-Iroquois father—voice filled with splinters,
the longing to leave Jamaica.

Mulatto

Here beneath north moon I find you awake
Floundering like a fish for whom there is no
Rest. I want to ask you why you are here,
What this means for our world—the eyes
Like prairie glass, beige skin.
Mulatto. Mongrel.

                You don't know any more than I do
                Who you are in this southern world
                Of rainbow fish and negro people.
                When mother told me the stories,
                She cried as if it were happening
                Again:

                              This is the way a black girl
                              navigates the black world.

Before I lost my curls to lye,
scrubbed my skin raw to be
just one damn shade lighter,
mother warned me of these
things. The world from which
we come never obliges
the either/or.

Down at the Crossroads
With Regards to Gwendolyn Brooks

Down at the crossroads,
we drink and we dance.
We live in the moment,
we bask in the past.
Time flies by us.
Youth's flower passes.
Still we down at the crossroads
drinkin' and dancin'.

Azuza Woman

Great grandmother groans
as she looks up at the sky
spread out on top of her,
gray wasteland, worried
feathers, swathed in strobes
of sun.

    More rain she thinks to herself.

On this edge of coast
love crashing into cliffs
as diffident and wide
as the shoulders she has missed,
she cannot breathe. The heat
has found her flaw.

    Nothing. She thinks. *No thing.*

Because each year brings
a new wrinkle, a new head-
stone. And now she understands
that she never had a chance.
That the wind itself
is a lie.

Sestina

Each year the road home
Is less, feels colder, more foreign.
The fairy-dust eaves and hedgerows fall
In gloom to greedy north stars and jezebel moons.
And our scars are comforted by distance,
The shades of purple autumn we know well.

At noon, the river brings stories of well-
Kept fishermen—men who now miss home,
Long to be united with the robin's egg distance,
A phenomenal stretch of bright opaline, foreign
Now to the men they were only days ago; men now moon-
Drunk and fierce. Soon, they will fall.

The breeze is pregnant with the scent of elms and river fish. This fall
families gather beneath the guise of late evening, at the old stone well,
Dry now but for dream catchings, slivers of moon
Isinglass tarot cards that speak of home:
A thing inextricably bound to the skins of weeping things—foreign
To all who linger on borders, hungry for the distance.

Bells toll in a long cacophony, every sound as distant
From the other as sea from sky, like poppy-seed sand as it falls,
Lost among caveats and sea-coast rocks, like the foreign
In lands they were pressed into by fear, grieved well-
Past the possible, finagled into a human home-
Stripped and starving for the voice of a goddess moon.

Tonight, like any other, our moon
Calls across the midnight veil, searching for the distant.
Time now for a crawl-space sky; time for *home,*
A pink ribbon on the earth's floor after darkness has fallen,
Given up its pearls and jewels as farewells
To the foreign.

We gather now in a place forgotten, foreign
Even, beneath the silent clatter of stilling life, a swelling moon
Above us. Tomorrow we will dig another well,

Deeper this time. Fill it with more water, stretch ourselves across more
distance. Internally beguiled and minute, like the men who have fallen
Into shadows of steel gray and cannot return home.

They are foreign to us now, these men who come home,
Who smell of moonshine and fallen stars. They ask us only for more
distance. A place at the well we have built for ourselves.

Pseudonym

From porch edge the South
looks like a ball of yarn:
unraveled, stalk thin layers
of purple bourbon and peanut
toffee.

      The ceiling is horse-shoed
in pewter shades, just dark enough
to hide your face as you read
the posthumously published private
lives of Gulfport Society.

Artimus, who is done stringing
her bow, is kneeling to Luther's
Saint Ana—painting
the virgin's fingernails.
Without hesitation

                Mother Moon
says that the South is one big
Babylon (and by the way, so are
Artimus and St. Ana). And by
all means,

Tell it to go to hell.

Etta Sings the Blues

Etta James could sing blues like crickets sang
Mississippi summer: with a half skunked pride,

A cool white stripe that could make Louisiana
Bayous feel like home.

When Etta sang the blues, white folks thought
We could finally do something right (though we still

Belonged in the cotton fields). But once, Etta sang
The blues and missed the whitest note of all—by one

Half step. All over Edenton, white folks screamed:
Niggers can't do nothin' right.

Now we're blue because our voice wasn't shrill enough.
Our fire was yellow instead of burnt-orange flame.

Our last ember burned itself from inside out, plunged
Headfirst into Soho where black folks were prohibited

But blues were allowed—and Etta's one flawed note
Became Mississippi cotton: Alabama moonshine:

A sepulchered doorway.

Hymn for Defilee

The scent itself is jazzy, full
as a blue-tick muffled by strands

of juniper, seeping drops of summer.
This is all there is you think, lying

on a flat rendering of sunlit grass. As if
you had never known the heat down

here is scorching, the snakes more poisonous,
the sky more pregnant. You can't

breathe for the humidity, black water
filling your lungs, tightening the noose.

You sing slave songs without notice. Songs
you learned from your grandmother,

and she from her mother. Now you know that loss
is genetic. Passed down through each jagged

world you've stretched through. You know
that your back pressed against the prickly grass

is un-original. *Done before.* Such is everything
in the world you come from. You cannot

change this repetition anymore than you can scrape
a midnight sky of the purple veil that comes before

the saddest rendition of storm. It owes you the world,
this sky, but won't let you taste it.

Acknowledgements

The author wishes to thank the editors of the following publications in which some of the poems herein first appeared, some in slightly different forms:

Chopper: "Harlem Manifesto"
Expressionists Magazine of the Arts: "Gravity" and "Tanque"
Review Americana: "West Cape, In Memoriam"
Rose & Thorn: "Peach Tree" and "Elegy in Broken Stanzas"
South Jersey Underground: "Art" and "Mulatto"

Many thanks to those who have inspired, sustained, and loved: Tom Shadyac, Stacy Rothberg, Marie Thomas. To Randall Wallace for gentility and hope; Angela Yarbrough for carving a road through despair; John Struloeff for guidance and counsel; David Holmes for depth and strength; Stewart Davenport for humor and excellent historical tutelage; Dr. Andrew K. Benton for his graciousness; Marnie Mitze for such undeserved compassion.

Thanks also to mother and father; Elainea Ashford; Verika Dildy.

Thanks to Candace, the most wonderful friend; and to Shun who manages, always, to keep things still.

Thanks to grandmother, from whom and for whom this book comes.

Finally, thanks to Leslie, a gem of a human being, and one hell of a writer.

www.ingramcontent.com/pod-product-compliance
Lightning Source LLC
Chambersburg PA
CBHW031214090426
42736CB00009B/910